My Australian Bird Book

by Heidi Damman

My Australian Bird Book

by Heidi Damman

Cockatoo

Magpie

Kookaburra

Budgie

Owl

Lorikeet

Eagle

Willy Wagtail

Duck

Galah

Emu

Cassowarry

Rosella

Fairy
Penguin

Download free colouring pages and interesting bird facts at: www.heididamman.com

OTHER TITLES

by

Heidi Damman

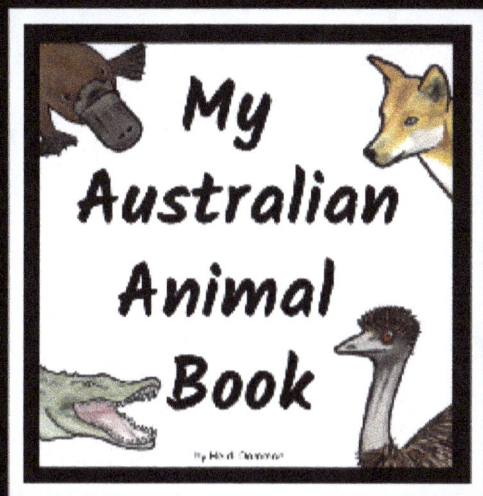

My Australian Animal Book

By Heidi Damman

www.ingramcontent.com/pod-product-compliance
Lightning Source LLC
Chambersburg PA
CBHW051618030426
42334CB00030B/3244